Welcome to
BOSNIA and
HERZEGOVINA

Gareth Stevens Publishing
A WORLD ALMANAC EDUCATION GROUP COMPANY

Written by
UMAIMA MULLA-FEROZE/MATILDA GABRIELPILLAI

Edited in USA by
DOROTHY L. GIBBS

Designed by
JAILANI BASARI

Picture research by
SUSAN JANE MANUEL

First published in North America in 2002 by
Gareth Stevens Publishing
A World Almanac Education Group Company
330 West Olive Street, Suite 100
Milwaukee, Wisconsin 53212 USA

Please visit our web site at:
www.garethstevens.com
For a free color catalog describing
Gareth Stevens' list of high-quality books
and multimedia programs, call
1-800-542-2595 (USA) or
1-800-461-9120 (CANADA).
Gareth Stevens Publishing's
Fax: (414) 332-3567.

© **TIMES MEDIA PRIVATE LIMITED 2002**
Originated and designed by
Times Editions
An imprint of Times Media Private Limited
A member of the Times Publishing Group
Times Centre, 1 New Industrial Road
Singapore 536196
http://www.timesone.com.sg/te

Library of Congress Cataloging-in-Publication Data
Mulla-Feroze, Umaima.
Welcome to Bosnia and Herzegovina / Umaima Mulla-Feroze
and Matilda Gabrielpillai.
p. cm. — (Welcome to my country)
Includes bibliographical references and index.
Summary: An overview of the geography, history, government,
economy, people, and culture of Bosnia and Herzegovina.
ISBN 0-8368-2529-2 (lib. bdg.)
1. Bosnia and Herzegovina—Juvenile literature. [1. Bosnia and
Herzegovina.] I. Gabrielpillai, Matilda. II. Title. III. Series.
DR1660.M85   2002
949.742—dc21   2001040622

Printed in Malaysia

1 2 3 4 5 6 7 8 9 06 05 04 03 02

PICTURE CREDITS
A.N.A. Press Agency: 26 (top), 33, 37
Archive Photos: 15, 16
Robert Bremac: 28, 36, 38, 45
Bruce Coleman Collection: 3 (center), 9
Evergreen Photo Alliance: Cover, 1, 3 (top),
    20, 21, 22, 29, 32, 34
Focus Team — Italy: 7
Simeon Glumac: 39
The Hutchison Library: 5
North Wind Picture Archives: 10
Topham Picturepoint: 3 (bottom), 6, 12,
    13, 30
Trip Photographic Library: 2, 4, 8, 14, 17,
    18, 19, 23, 24, 25, 26 (bottom), 27, 31,
    35, 40, 41, 43
Vision Photo Agency: 11

Digital Scanning by Superskill Graphics Pte Ltd

Contents

Words that appear in the glossary are printed in **boldface** type the first time they occur in the text.

Welcome to Bosnia and Herzegovina!

Bosnia and Herzegovina is sometimes simply called Bosnia, but the country has two **distinct** regions. Bosnia is in the north. Herzegovina is in the south. Let's explore beautiful Bosnia and learn about its history and its people.

Opposite: The Neretva River is just one example of Herzegovina's natural beauty.

Below: Bosnia's capital, Sarajevo, is the country's most **cosmopolitan** city.

The Flag of Bosnia & Herzegovina

The flag adopted in 1998 has a yellow triangle on a blue background. The triangle's points stand for Bosnia's three main **ethnic** groups. The stars represent the Council of Europe. The half stars represent Bosnia's two regions.

The Land

Bosnia has an area of 19,781 square miles (51,233 square kilometers). It is on the Balkan **Peninsula**, which is the largest European peninsula on the Mediterranean Sea. The countries of Serbia and Montenegro border Bosnia on the east and the southeast. Except for a very short southwestern coastline on the Adriatic Sea, the rest of the country is surrounded by Croatia. The capital city of Bosnia is Sarajevo.

Below: This steep waterfall on the Vrbas River is near the town of Jajce.

Mountain ranges stretch across southern and western Bosnia, and the Dinaric Alps form a natural western border with Croatia. At 7,828 feet (2,386 meters), Mount Maglic, on the southeastern border, is Bosnia's highest peak. Herzegovina, Bosnia's southern region, has dry limestone **plateaus** rising as high as 6,562 feet (2,000 m). Bosnia's major rivers are the Bosna, Drina, Sava, Una, and Vrbas in the north and the Neretva in the south.

Above:
Magnificent cliffs border the banks of the Neretva River in the southern region of Herzegovina.

Climate

The Dinaric Alps shelter Bosnia from the Adriatic Sea, keeping its climate **moderate**. In the northern city of Banja Luka, temperatures are about 32° Fahrenheit (0° Celsius) in winter and 72° F (22° C) in summer. Mostar, in the south, has temperatures ranging from 43° F (6° C) to 100° F (38° C).

Above: Northern Bosnia gets a lot of snow in winter. Patches of snow are still on the ground even at the end of the season.

Plants and Animals

Beech, oak, and pine forests are abundant in Bosnia's fertile northern region. Even the dry southern region of Herzegovina has areas where fig and cypress trees thrive.

Bosnia's wildlife includes a variety of animals, such as wolves, wildcats, otters, falcons, foxes, and Herzegovinian bears.

Left: The European wildcat is normally a shy animal, but it can be fierce when it is scared or if it feels threatened.

History

The Illyrians were the first people known to settle in the area that is now Bosnia. The Romans conquered most of Bosnia in the first century A.D., and the powerful Serbs and Croats from Central Europe ruled from the seventh century to the twelfth century.

Left: The Illyrians were settled in the western part of the Balkan Peninsula by the seventh century B.C.

From 1180 to 1463, Hungary controlled Bosnia, and the country was governed by **viceroys** called *bans* (BAHNS). Ban Stjepan Kotromanic, who reigned from 1322 to 1353,

conquered Herzegovina (then called Hum), uniting the two regions until Herzegovina broke away in 1448.

The Turks captured Bosnia in 1463 and Herzegovina in 1483, making both regions provinces of the Ottoman Empire. Peasant unrest in 1875 and war with Russia in 1877 led international powers to decide that the Austro-Hungarian Empire should take over in Bosnia.

Left: Archduke Franz Ferdinand, heir to the Austro-Hungarian throne, visited Sarajevo in 1914 with his wife, Sophie. They were both killed by an **assassin** during this visit.

The Rise and Fall of Yugoslavia

Because Serbia and Croatia wanted to control Bosnia and establish the independent state of Yugoslavia, Austria-Hungary **annexed** Bosnia in 1908. In 1914, Gavrilo Princip, a Bosnian Serb, killed the heir to the Austro-Hungarian throne. Austria-Hungary responded by declaring war on Serbia, which started World War I.

When the war ended in 1918, the Austro-Hungarian Empire broke apart. Bosnia became part of the Kingdom of Serbs, Croats, and Slovenes, which was renamed Yugoslavia in 1929.

In the 1940s, during World War II, Germany occupied part of Yugoslavia, including Bosnia. Josip Broz Tito, a Croatian, led a **resistance movement** that freed Bosnia from the Germans in 1945. Bosnia then became part of a communist-ruled Yugoslav federation, which also included Croatia, Serbia, Herzegovina, Montenegro, Slovenia, Kosovo, Vojvodina, and Macedonia. Tito was its president. When Tito died in 1980, the federation fell apart.

Below: General Josip Broz Tito reviews Yugoslav soldiers in 1944. The Yugoslav army was powerful, even after Tito's death.

The Ethnic War of 1992–1995

In 1992, Bosnia and Herzegovina claimed independence, but a horrible ethnic war followed. Serbs wanted to reunite all of the Yugoslav territories but **eliminate** all non-Serbian people. The Serbian army attacked Sarajevo and other Bosnian towns, **persecuting** or killing non-Serbs. Peace talks in 1995, divided Bosnia into the Serb Republika Srpska and the Federation of Bosnia and Herzegovina.

Above: Much of Sarajevo had to be rebuilt after the war of 1992–1995.

Ban Kulin (r. 1180–1204)

Although *ban* is a title normally given by Hungarian kings, Ban Kulin took it for himself. During his reign, he freed Bosnia from Hungary, expanded its territory, and brought peace and prosperity.

King Tvrtko I (1338–1391)

Bosnia's first king and greatest ruler, Tvrtko I, made his country the most powerful state in the Balkans. Conquests made during his reign increased Bosnia's land. By 1390, Bosnia included parts of Croatia, Slovenia, and Montenegro.

Alija Izetbegovic (1925–)

A member of the Muslim Party of Democratic Action, Alija Izetbegovic was elected President of Bosnia in 1990. With the leaders of Serbia and Croatia, he signed the peace agreement that ended the ethnic war of 1992–1995.

Alija Izetbegovic

Government and the Economy

The current system of government in Bosnia was established by the 1995 peace agreement that divided the country into the Serbian Republic, or

Left: A conference on Bosnia, in 1998, brought together leaders of more than fifty countries. The members of Bosnia's **tripartite** presidency who attended were Croat Ante Jelavic (*left*), Serb Zivko Radisic (*center*), and Bosniak Alija Izetbegovic (*right*).

Republika Srpska, and the Federation of Bosnia and Herzegovina. Both the Republic and the Federation each have a local president and a **parliament**.

The central government has three presidents, one elected from each of the three main ethnic groups — Serbs, Bosniaks, and Croats. This tripartite presidency appoints a Council of Ministers in charge of foreign policy, trade, and other national issues.

Left: Peacekeeping is an international effort in Bosnia. The Stabilization Force (SFOR) is made up of troops from more than thirty nations.

The United Nations, the United States, and the European Union, all played a role in Bosnia's peace talks and are active in its government.

The Economy

The war of 1992–1995 destroyed Bosnia's economy. Industries stopped producing, and many people lost their jobs. Since 1995, the country has been reconstructing cities, power lines, and telecommunication and transportation systems. More people have jobs again, but 40 percent are still unemployed.

Left:
One of Bosnia's successes after the war of 1992–1995 was to establish a single, central bank. The Central Bank building (*left*) is in Sarajevo.

Before the war, agriculture and Bosnia's rich mineral resources, such as **bauxite**, iron, coal, and zinc, contributed more than half of the country's wealth. Today, education, transportation, banking, and health care services are more important.

In 1998, Bosnia introduced major banking and finance **reforms** and established a national currency, the convertible mark. Bosnia still needs international aid and loans. With a recovering economy, however, it will need less foreign aid in the future.

People and Lifestyle

The people of Bosnia belong to many ethnic groups, but almost all of them are **descendants** of the South Slav people who settled in the western Balkans in the seventh century. The three main ethnic groups are Serbs, Bosniaks, and Croats.

Minority groups in Bosnia include the Romany, who are descendants of **nomadic** people from India, and Jews. Together, these minorities are only 7 percent of Bosnia's population.

Below: Home for this Bosniak family is a village close to the city of Sarajevo.

Left: Sarajevo has a youth club that is open to Bosnian children of all ethnic groups. At this club, children learn, through art, how to deal with the **trauma** of war.

Serbs, Bosniaks, and Croats

Ethnic identity is very important to Bosnians. Approximately 40 percent of the population is Serb, 38 percent is Bosniak, and 17 percent is Croat. After the war of 1992–1995, Bosnia was divided into two regions. Serbs occupy the region known today as Republika Srpska. The Bosniaks and the Croats live in the Federation of Bosnia and Herzegovina. Very few areas have a mixture of ethnic groups.

Family Life

The home and family are the heart of Bosnian life, but the war destroyed Bosnian homes and separated family members. Some have still not found their loved ones. For those who survived the war, life now revolves around providing a better future for their children.

Left:
Family values have a strong influence on social activities in Bosnia. Family members spend a lot of time together.

Some survivors of the war had to rebuild their homes. Others had to rebuild their lives. Forced out of their homes, towns, and villages, they had to find new, "safe" communities with members of their own ethnic group. Many moved from country villages to find work in the cities. Yet, city or country, family ties remain strong.

Education

When Bosnia was in the Yugoslav federation, **illiteracy**, especially among women and in rural areas, was high. Steps taken in the 1990s to improve the country's education system suffered a setback when schools became targets in the war of 1992–1995. Today, schools are being repaired or rebuilt.

Above: Most of the children in Bosnia start school at the age of seven. All Bosnian children must attend primary school.

In Bosnia, children attend eight years of primary school and four years of secondary school. Many also attend religious classes held at a **mosque** or a church.

Bosnia has four universities. The University of Sarajevo, built in 1949, is the oldest and largest. The others are in Mostar, Tuzla, and Banja Luka.

Left: Some of the secondary schools in Bosnia have computer facilities for their students. This computer room is at a school in Sarajevo.

Religion

Bosnia's constitution gives citizens the freedom to practice any religion. In reality, however, people can safely practice a faith only where that faith is the main religion.

Bosnia has three main religions, and religion and ethnic identity are closely related. Serbs are usually Eastern Orthodox Christians. Most Bosniaks are Muslims. Croats are usually Roman Catholics. A small number of Bosnians are Jews or Protestants or belong to other faiths.

Above: Catholics living in Sarajevo attend the Cathedral of Jesus' Heart.

Left: These Muslim men are reading the Qur'an, the Islamic holy book, at a mosque in Mostar. Islam has many followers in Bosnia.

During communist rule, religion was discouraged in Bosnia. Today, young Bosnians, especially the Croats in Herzegovina, seem to be returning to religion. Among Muslim Bosniaks, however, most do not strictly follow Islamic rules. Bosniak women, for example, do not wear veils.

Left: The design of a Serb Orthodox church, such as this one in Sarajevo, is similar to other Eastern Orthodox churches. The inside is usually decorated with scenes from the Bible, such as the Last Supper.

Language

Bosnians have one common language, Serbo-Croatian. It has been used since the twelfth century. During Ottoman rule, however, about six thousand Turkish words found their way into this South Slav language.

Today, Bosniaks call the language Bosnian, Croats call it Croatian, and Serbs call it Serbian. Bosniaks and Croats write the language in Roman script. Serbs use **Cyrillic** script. Any educated Bosnian can read both scripts.

Left: This sign reads "Welcome to Republic of Srpska" in Cyrillic script. This script was invented in the ninth century by a Greek monk named Cyril.

Left:
Books that were rescued from stores destroyed in the war of 1992–1995 are now showing up in bookstalls on the streets of Sarajevo.

Literature

Bosnia's literature reflects a mixture of cultures, including Slav, Turkish, Greek, Arabic, and European. For example, a form of Bosnian poetry, called Aljamiado literature, has Arab and Spanish influences.

Folk poetry is one of the country's most important literary forms. The sad love poem *Hasanaganica*, or *The Wife of Hasan Aga*, became one of the most popular folk poems in Europe and was translated by famous European writers, such as Lord Byron of England, into their own languages.

Arts

Architecture

The buildings in Bosnia combine Islamic, European, Roman, Gothic, and other similar architectural styles. Many buildings were damaged or destroyed in the war of 1992–1995. In restoring and rebuilding them, Bosnians are trying to preserve their architectural **heritage**.

Left: One of the remaining stone fortresses built by the Ottoman Turks overlooks a town in Herzegovina.

Bosnia still has some of the spectacular mosques and impressive stone fortresses built by the Ottoman Turks. Ottoman architecture often had Christian elements, such as tall, narrow stained-glass windows.

Mosques throughout the country also have beautifully carved wooden staircases. Wood carving is an ancient craft in Bosnia. Traditionally, houses were built almost entirely of wood and furniture was elaborately carved.

Above: This house in Mostar was built in the seventeenth century. Its **ornate** wooden furniture is elaborately carved with geometric and floral designs.

Traditional Crafts

During Turkish rule, many Bosnian craftspeople were skilled in the arts of calligraphy, miniature painting, manuscript **illumination**, and leather book binding, which were all part of producing books. Book binding is still a strong tradition in Sarajevo.

Carpet weaving is another ancient craft. The Persians, who were master carpet weavers, were responsible for developing this art in Bosnia. Today, the carpets produced in each different town have their own unique design.

Left: A beautifully designed Bosnian carpet hangs outside a shop in Mostar. Other centers of carpet manufacturing in Bosnia are the cities of Foča, Stolac, Gacko, Visegrad, and Sarajevo.

Elegant fabrics and embroidered pillowcases and cushion covers are also part of Bosnia's artistic tradition. Textile manufacturing is a leading industry, producing valuable fabrics, such as velvet and brocade.

Bosnia is well-known for its metalwork, too. Techniques such as **engraving**, **embossing**, **encrustation**, and **filigree** are used in decorating metal jewelry and household utensils.

Above:
This craftsman is embossing a metal container at his studio in Sarajevo. Most metalworkers in Sarajevo specialize in embossing and engraving. Banja Luka has the best filigree workers.

Leisure

Bosnians are warm, friendly people. In rural villages, neighbors often visit each other just to chat. These visits are called *ide na kafu* (ih-deh nah KAH-FOO), or coffee visits. Village women often meet to exchange news. Special events, such as weddings, birthdays, and homecomings, are also occasions for visiting. Rural Bosnians like to entertain each other by telling stories.

Left: Leisure time in rural areas of Bosnia is often spent enjoying coffee with family and friends.

Embroidery is another popular pastime for rural women. Many ethnic groups can be identified by the distinct patterns of embroidery on their clothes.

Urban Bosnians enjoy spending time with family and friends, too. They like to go shopping, meet at a café, go to a movie, or walk in the park. Reading and embroidery are popular indoor activities.

Above:
In Bosnian cities, in-line skating and riding bicycles are popular outdoor activities.

Left: Sarajevo's Mount Bjelasnica was the site of skiing events in the 1984 Winter Olympics.

Sports

The mountains, rivers, and wildlife in Bosnia have helped determine some of the country's favorite sports and outdoor activities. In winter, Bosnians go cross-country skiing, ice-skating, and sledding. Children in the cities even sled down snow-covered streets.

Hunting is a major sport in early summer, and the huge Herzegovinian brown bear is a special challenge for hunters. This plant-eating bear is so strong it can uproot trees.

Bosnia's lakes Jablanicko Jezero and Busko Jezero are known as the best fishing spots in the region. The country's rocky mountain ranges and thick forests are a thrill for hikers.

The most popular team sports in Bosnia are soccer and basketball. The country has three soccer leagues and two basketball leagues. The national soccer team took fourth place in its group in the qualifying round for the Euro 2000 soccer championships.

Below: Bosnian teenagers often get together for neighborhood soccer games, especially in the summertime.

Festivals

With three major religions, Bosnians celebrate many religious festivals, and they also participate in festivals that are not part of any particular religion.

Bajram is a three-day Muslim festival celebrated immediately after Ramadan, the Muslim month of **fasting**. Muslims also celebrate the anniversaries of their mosques.

Left: Strings of colorful electric lights decorate the Gazi Husrev-Bey mosque in Sarajevo during the Muslim festival of Bajram.

Krsna Slava honors the spiritual birthday of the Serbian people. Each family holds this festival on the day their family or tribe was first baptized into the Eastern Orthodox Church.

Above: Families celebrate Krsna Slava at an Eastern Orthodox church. Bread prepared as an offering to thank God for his blessings is part of the ceremony.

More than half of all Bosnians celebrate Christmas, but all regions do not celebrate the same way. Serbs decorate a *badnjak* (BAHD-nyak), or Christmas tree, with ribbons, fruits, nuts, and candies, and they put straw under it to symbolize Christ's manger.

Food

Bosnian cooking combines the flavors of the Mediterranean, Central Europe, the Balkans, and the Middle East.

Cevapcici (CHAY-VAHP-chee-chee) is seasoned lamb, pork, or beef sausage that is grilled with onions and served on thick pita bread. *Bosanski lonac* (BOSS-ahn-skee LON-atz) is Bosnian hotpot stew. It is a delicious mixture of slowly roasted meat and vegetables served in its cooking pot.

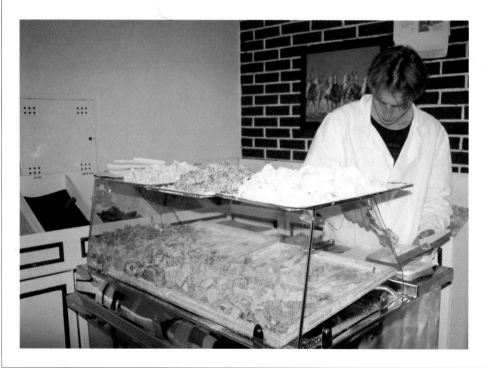

Left: Bosnians eat an assortment of sweets, including Turkish delight, a gummy, jellylike candy that is cut into cubes and dusted with sugar. This candy comes in many different flavors, with or without nuts.

The Ottoman Turks introduced stuffed vegetables. Ground meat, rice, spices, and chopped vegetables are wrapped in cabbage leaves, or stuffed inside hollowed-out peppers, potatoes, or onions, and cooked slowly in a tightly covered dish over an open fire.

Baklava (buck-LAAVA) is a popular pastry dessert with a sweet filling of chopped nuts and honey.

Above: This market in Sarajevo offers a variety of fruits, including grapes, apples, plums, pomegranates, and pears. Bosnia is known for its "Turkish plums," called damsons.

BOSNIA AND HERZEGOVINA

SLOVENIA

HUNGARY

Sava

Vojvodina

Danube

Sava

BELGRAD

Una

●Banja Luka

Vrbas

Bosna

Tuzla
●

B O S N I A (region)

Jajce
●

Bosna

Drina

Serbia

CROATIA

YUGOSLAVIA

Busko
Jezero

Jablanicko
Jezero

SARAJEVO ■

Visegrad
●

D a l m a t i a n

HERZEGOVINA
(region)

Foča
●

Neretva

Mount Maglic
7,828 ft / 2,386 m

Mostar
●

Stolac
●

Gacko
●

M o n t e n e g r o

C o a s t

Kosov

State Boundary

Regional Boundary

Entity Boundary

Republika Srpska

**Federation of Bosnia
and Herzegovina**

■ **Capital**

● **City**

River

N

ADRIATIC SEA

ALBANIA

42

Above: The Old Town area of Sarajevo is a historic part of the city.

Adriatic Sea A3–C5
Albania D5

Banja Luka B2
Belgrade
    (Serbia) D2
Bosna River C2–C3
Bosnia (region)
    A2–C4
Busko Jezero
    (lake) B3

Croatia A1–C5

Dalmatian Coast
    A3–C4
Danube River
    C1–D2
Dinaric Alps A2–D5
Drina River D2–C4

Federation of
    Bosnia and
    Herzegovina
    A2–C4
Foča C3

Gacko C4

Herzegovina
    (region) B3–C4
Hungary B1–C1

Jablanicko Jezero
    (lake) B3
Jajce B3

Kosovo D4–D5

Montenegro C4–D5
Mostar B4
Mount Maglic C4

Neretva River
    B4–C4
Republika Srpska
    A2–C4
Sarajevo C3
Sava River A1–D2
Serbia D2–D4
Slovenia A1

Stolac B4
Tuzla C2

Una River A3–B2

Visegrad D3
Vojvodina C1-D2
Vrbas River B2–B3

Yugoslavia C1–D5

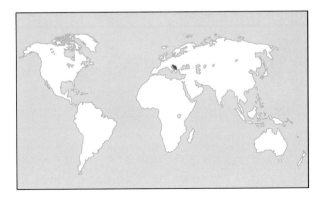

Quick Facts

Official Name   Bosnia and Herzegovina

Capital   Sarajevo

Official Language   Serbo-Croatian (Bosnian, Croatian, or Serbian)

Population   3,835,777 (2000 estimate)

Land Area   19,781 square miles (51,233 square km)

Administrative Divisions   Federation of Bosnia and Herzegovina, Republika Srpska

Highest Point   Mount Maglic 7,828 feet (2,386 m)

Major Rivers   Bosna, Drina, Neretva, Sava, Una, Vrbas

Main Religions   Eastern Orthodox Christianity, Islam, Roman Catholicism

Main Ethnic Groups   Bosniaks, Croats, Serbs

Currency   Convertible Mark (2.193 BAK = U.S. $1 as of 2001)

Opposite: The town of Jajce rises above this beautiful waterfall on the Vrbas River.

Glossary

annexed: added a country or territory to the existing territory of the controlling country or state.

assassin: a person who murders a government leader.

bauxite: the material from which aluminum is made.

cosmopolitan: having an international appearance and worldwide appeal.

descendants: the line of people born within a certain family or culture of ancestors.

distinct: different in a noticeable way.

eliminate: get rid of.

embossing: decorating with a design that is raised above the surface.

encrustation: the design technique of filling in carvings with silver, gold, or pearl.

engraving: lightly carving figures or designs into a solid surface.

ethnic: related to a certain race or culture of people.

fasting: not eating food for a certain period of time.

filigree: the art of making delicate designs by twisting fine wire.

heritage: the styles and practices passed down by earlier generations.

illiteracy: the inability to read or write due to a lack of education.

illumination: the art of decorating books or manuscripts with silver, gold, or brilliant colors and designs.

moderate: not extreme.

mosque: a churchlike place where Muslims go to pray.

nomadic: wandering or moving around without having a permanent home.

ornate: having a lot of decoration.

parliament: a group of elected government representatives who make the laws for their country.

peninsula: a long piece of land that is surrounded by water on three sides.

persecuting: treating cruelly, and often torturing, because of race, religion, culture, or political beliefs.

plateaus: large areas of high, flat land that rise sharply above the land around them.

reforms: changes or improvements, usually to correct problems.

resistance movement: an organized effort to oppose and change an existing government.

trauma: severe emotional shock.

tripartite: made up of three parties.

viceroys: people who govern a province or a colony as a representative of the ruler of another country.

More Books to Read

Bosnia: Can There Ever Be Peace?
Topics in the News series. David
Flint (Raintree/Steck-Vaughn)

Bosnia: Civil War in Europe. Children
in Crisis series. Keith Greenberg
(Blackbirch Marketing)

Bosnia: The Struggle for Peace. Sherry
Ricciardi (Millbrook Press)

A Bosnian Family. Journey Between Two
Worlds series. Robin Landew
Silverman (Lerner)

A Family from Bosnia. Families Around
the World series. Julia Waterlow
(Raintree/Steck-Vaughn)

Smiling for Strangers. Gaye Hicyilmaz
(Farrar, Straus & Giroux)

Young People from Bosnia Talk about
War. Issues in Focus series. Harvey
and Bryna J. Fireside (Enslow)

Zlata's Diary: A Child's Life in
Sarajevo. Zlata Filipovic
(Econo-Clad Books)

Videos

Escape from Bosnia: The Scott
O'Grady Story — Escape!
(A & E Home Video)

Jugoslavia: Adriatic Coast.
(Education 2000)

Web Sites

www.abcnews.go.com/sections/
world/balkans_content/
balkans_whoswho.html

www.infoplease.com/ipa/
A0107349.html

www.odci.gov/cia/publications/
factbook/geos/bk.html

www.oxfam.org.uk/coolplanet/
kidsweb/world/Bosnia/
boshome.htm

Due to the dynamic nature of the Internet, some web sites stay current longer than others. To find additional web sites, use a reliable search engine with one or more of the following keywords to help you locate information about Bosnia. Keywords: *Balkans, Bosnia, Croatia, Alija Izetbegovic, Mostar, Serbia, Sarajevo.*

Index